Paper and Board

CW00816215

. . . .

Fire safety in the paper and board industry

HSE BOOKS

© Crown copyright 1995
First published 1995
Applications for reproduction should be made to HMSO

ISBN 0 7176 0841 7

CONTENTS

INTRODUCTION

1   In the paper and board industry management of risk arising from fire hazards is a critical part of any manager's job. This guidance is aimed at managers who have responsibility for fire safety to help them fulfil their duties under the Fire Precautions Act 1971, the Health and Safety at Work etc Act 1974 and other relevant legislation. It will also be useful to engineering management, health and safety advisers, trainers, technical staff, supervisors, safety representatives and everyone working in the industry.

2   This guidance advises on good practice directed at minimising the outbreak and spread of fire and ensuring the safety of personnel in the event of fire. References are made to some standards of protection which are higher than those which would be required by law for the protection of personnel. Managers have to take into account asset protection, including the requirements of their insurance companies, and the resulting fire prevention and precautionary measures will reflect this combined approach.

3   Paper and board are combustible. While solid blocks of paper may not be easily ignited, once they have caught fire flames can spread rapidly and be difficult to extinguish. Loose paper, shrink wrap material and flammable liquids or gases can ignite easily and spread the fire to other materials. High temperature steam pipes can, if not properly insulated, be a cause of fire in insulation or other combustible material.

4   The fire service is called every year to a number of fires in the paper and board industry. In some incidents people have been injured and there is always the potential for multiple fatalities. In many others there has been extensive damage to buildings, equipment and materials; in addition to the immediate material damage there are inevitably consequential losses, such as plant, customers, possibly jobs, and dispersal of skilled staff. For summaries of some fires in the industry see Appendix 1. Although malicious acts have had a lot of publicity and caused extensive damage, a recent survey has shown that these only caused 7% of fires reported to the local authority fire brigade. Machine faults and poor housekeeping were the cause of over 60% of fires.

5   In some firms small fires frequently occur without any significant damage or downtime. There is a tendency for these to be regarded as a normal part of the process but it must be realised that these small fires can spread. The incidence of such fires should be included in the assessment of fire hazard.

6   The risk of a fire breaking out in a particular place and spreading rapidly will depend largely upon the materials being used and stored, the general standards of housekeeping, the construction and layout of the factory and the training of employees. The risk to people after a fire has started will largely depend on the adequacy and maintenance of means of escape and of the alarm system and the training of the workforce in fire routine and evacuation

. . . .

procedures. Adequate controls should ensure that:

(a) the risk of fire occurring is reduced to the absolute minimum;

(b) the risk of fire spreading is minimised; and

(c) everyone is able by their own unaided efforts to reach a place of safety beyond the building (see paragraph 21(c) for the needs of people with disabilities).

7   There should be consultation with insurers about fire precautions, especially before any changes in the building or process activity which could affect the spread of fire.

LEGAL REQUIREMENTS

8   There are a number of legal requirements which are relevant to the prevention of fire in the paper and board industry. Appendix 2 gives details of these requirements. The advice in this guidance is supported by the Home Office, the Scottish Home and Health Department and the Health and Safety Executive (HSE) and is relevant whatever legislation applies.

9   In paper and board mills HSE enforces those precautions required in connection with the use and storage of flammable substances and in connection with processes involving significant fire hazards. They are generally referred to as 'process fire precautions'. The Fire Authority enforces the precautions required to ensure the safety of persons after the outbreak of fire. These precautions include provision of means of escape and the means of ensuring that they can be safely and effectively used; fire warning systems; first aid; fire-fighting equipment; and procedures for action to be taken in the event of fire, including instruction and training of staff. They are referred to as 'general fire precautions'.

10   The terms 'general fire precautions' and 'process fire precautions' overlap and may affect each other in practice. For example, the means for fighting fire which are required in connection with the keeping and use of flammable substances will also form part of the general fire precautions of the building. However, the general fire precautions in the building may be affected by the presence of the flammable substances and, for example, additional means of escape in case of fire may be necessary.

CAUSES OF FIRES

11   In order for fires to start and spread there needs to be fuel, oxygen and a source of ignition:

. . . .

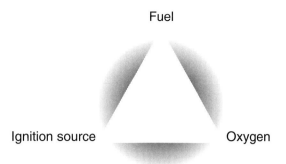

Fuel

Ignition source   Oxygen

Figure 1

12   In paper mills there is always paper and paper dust. Both of these are readily ignitable fuels. In addition there may be other flammable solids (eg shrink wrap plastic), flammable liquids (eg oil, solvents etc) and flammable gases (eg liquefied petroleum gas in cylinders or hydrogen sulphide generated by the process).

13   Oxygen is always available from the air.

14   Sources of ignition cannot be completely eliminated. They are likely to include:

(a)   frictional heating (eg hot bearings);

(b)   sparks (eg from hand tools);

(c)   static discharges;

(d)   naked flames (eg on welding equipment or gas fired plant);

(e)   electrical sources (eg overloaded conductors);

(f)   hot surfaces (eg steam pipes or infra-red dryers).

(g)   cigarettes and/or matches;

15   Both the fuel and sources of ignition should be controlled to minimise the risk of fire. Typically problems arise from the following situations:

(a)   poorly maintained equipment;

(b)   welding and/or cutting of plant;

(c)   faulty or misused electrical equipment;

(d) poor storage of packaging materials;

(e) poor storage or handling of flammable liquids and/or gases;

(f) inadequate site security.

(g) smoking and smoking materials;

16 Once started, fires can spread rapidly. The following will contribute to rapid fire spread:

(a) poor housekeeping and accumulation of waste material;

(b) unsegregated storage of materials increasing fire hazard;

(c) excessive stocks of paper in production areas;

(d) unbanded, end-stacked reels of paper;

(e) lack of fire separation between floors or rooms;

(f) fire doors wedged or propped open;

(g) combustibility and fire spread characteristics of wall and ceiling linings;

(h) poorly maintained fire fighting equipment.

(i) inadequate/inappropriate fire detection and extinguishing equipment;

(j) inadequate provision of fire venting;

17 The action of personnel also is critical to the spread of fire. If the wrong extinguishers are used or staff fail to follow appropriate instructions then the situation will be considerably worse than it need be. Where there is a mill fire team there should be a clear policy as to when the local authority fire brigade is called in.

FIRE RISK MANAGEMENT

18 Employers need to organise for fire safety and the appointment of a senior manager to be responsible for fire risk management and staff training is the initial step towards an effective action plan. Apart from the formal steps set out in paragraphs 19-21 successful fire risk management entails:

(a) constant and careful thought;

(b) an awareness of all the potential risks associated with the premises, its processes, the workforce and contractors;

(c) effective liaison with the fire authority (usually the local authority fire brigade);

(d) effective liaison with insurers.

19 An initial assessment of the risk of fires and the adequacy of the measures provided or needed to combat the risk should be carried out. This will be the type of assessment required by the Management of Health and Safety Regulations 1992. It involves consideration of two factors: identifying the fire hazards (ie materials that burn and ignition sources, unsatisfactory structural features etc) and then evaluating the fire risk (ie the likelihood that a fire will occur and the consequences of such a fire on the people present). The risk assessment should help in deciding what measures must be taken to provide suitable arrangements for protecing people in the workplace from fire, and should ensure that:

(a) the risk of fire occurring is reduced to the absolute minimum;

(b) the risk of fire spreading is minimised; and

(c) everyone at the workplace is able, without outside assistance, to reach a place of safety.

20 A range of key staff will be involved. They should consult with safety representatives in accordance with normal procedures. The significant features of a risk assessment are required to be recorded and the arrangements for controlling fire risk will form part of the overall company health and safety policy. These arrangements should be seen also as good management practices and need to clearly allocate the responsibilities of everyone involved in fire safety.

21 The following general issues need to be addressed:

(a) A full audit will be needed to identify all the hazards and risks together with existing control measures, including information provision and training. The audit should identify hazards arising from the materials and processes used, and indicate the risk of outbreak and spread of fire. A plan of the site may be helpful for recording findings. The audit may be done either on a process-by-process basis, eg materials delivery, materials storage, process A, intermediate storage, process B etc, or area-by-area. There should be definite conclusions about the level of hazard and risk, and decisions about the adequacy of protection and the need for improvement.

(b) Occasionally a fire will occur even in the best-run organisation. It is necessary to assume that it will, and plan accordingly. The arrangements should include written emergency arrangements. Where the assessment and, in particular, past experience indicates the types of fires which can be anticipated, specific plans to tackle these should be made. The emergency arrangements should specify the particular fire safety responsibilities of the most senior person present having overall control of the workplace, and specify the responsibilities of other nominated persons. The aim should be that, in the event of a fire, everybody in the workplace is sufficiently familiar with the fire routine and fire safety arrangements for the correct actions to be taken and the workplace to be safely evacuated. The planning can deal with not only ensuring the safety of employees but also with the implications for production. The arrangements could include the following steps: take each part of the process or plant in turn, assume it is out of commission and assess the potential for damage to production should a fire occur; can the process be done elsewhere; can alternative machinery be obtained.

(c) particular planning needs to be done for people with disabilities in the workplace. It is preferable for them to be able to leave the building in an emergency without help. This may need physical alterations to the premises or the provision of a suitable system whereby the help would be always available when needed. Further guidance is given in References 3 and 14.

Assessment 22 The following detailed steps will form part of the assessment:

General fire precautions

23 The main precautions are as follows:

(a) Find out whether a fire certificate already exists; if not, ask the fire authority whether a fire certificate is required and apply for one if necessary. If a fire certificate already exists check that it is up to date and all conditions are met;

(b) Have any material alterations taken place? If so, inform the fire authority immediately - you could be in breach of the law;

(c) Identify the existing means of escape and ensure these can be used safely;

(d) Check the arrangements for giving warning in case of fire (a fire alarm is a requirement in any building requiring a fire certificate);

(e) Identify the numbers, position and state of readiness of the portable fire extinguishers and/or hose reels;

(f) Are the fire evacuation drills being carried out and has the training been given as specified in the fire certificate?

(g) Do you have the record of training, fire equipment checks etc required by the certificate;

(h) Do small fires occur frequently, and are they taken for granted? If so are they investigated, what is the cause, and can they be eliminated? (It would be unusual if they could not.);

(i) Is there a need to provide information/signs in languages other than English?

Process hazards/risks and control measures

24 The main recommended measures are as follows:

(a) Examine the process layout and flow of materials;

(b) Identify materials that will burn readily. Make use of experience of previous incidents and the information which should be available from manufacturers and suppliers on their health and safety data sheets;

(c) Identify hazardous activities, eg those involving the generation of paper dust, welding and cutting, storage of paper reels;

(d) Review the arrangements for handling flammable liquids and controlling flammable vapours;

(e) Identify and control sources of ignition including any transient sources from cleaning, maintenance or repair work;

(f) Consider the amount of material both in storage and in use and where it is stored and used

(g) Identify conditions of fire spread, eg from storage to process areas and vice versa, and separate where necessary;

(h) Consider standards of housekeeping, waste removal and improve these as necessary;

(i) Consider the emergencies that might arise (including spills and leaks) and draw up appropriate procedures;

(j) Consider the activities of contractors and provide adequate controls, eg by preparing and enforcing rules for contractors doing hot work;

(k) Assess the adequacy of fences, doors etc, in keeping out children and other intruders;

(l) Review the need for preventive maintenance, eg lubrication, electrical checks etc so that hazards are minimised.

Investigation of incidents

25   It is essential that all fires or incidents giving rise to a risk of fire, eg spillage of highly flammable liquids (HFLs), overheated bearings, are thoroughly investigated and lessons learnt which are incorporated into the plan for the control of fire risk.

Consideration of additional control measures

26   Other control measures are:

(a)   Decide whether risks can be reduced by installing safer plant or by modifying existing plant;

(b)   Install fixed fire-fighting equipment where appropriate;

(c)   Plan what first-aid fire-fighting can be done by your own staff, paying particular attention to the types of fire you have experienced and can anticipate, eg fires inside machine drier hoods;

(d)   Control smoking;

(e)   Obtain expert fire advice prior to any material alteration to the premises or the processes carried on there;

(f)   Review the role of supervision in preventing fire and dealing with emergencies.

Training

27   A key element in management of fire risk is the provision of adequate supervision and training. Employees need to be informed about:

(a)   the process risks;

(b)   the standards to be maintained;

(c)   working practices to be adopted;

(d)   fire routine and evacuation procedures.

28   Develop a fire risk awareness among all employees by providing regular training in fire prevention and fire safety. During training on fire routines inform employees about why some things are done in relationship to fire precautionary measures, eg why fire doors should be kept shut, why fire alarm testing is done, etc. The best fire preventers are a well-trained and informed workforce.

....

29 The assessment should draw conclusions about the hazard and risk and identifying any additional control measures needed. It should also specify what monitoring needs to be carried out to maintain effective control of the risks.

Monitoring **30** Maintain standards by monitoring and measuring good practice and any improvements. Ensure that any shortcomings are corrected. Even though all employees should report any hazard that they notice, a system of regular formal inspection by management is necessary to monitor conditions and to identify changes that may introduce additional risks. The company safety policy should make it clear who carries out these inspections, and when. The results of the inspections should be recorded to aid assessment and reports at defined intervals made to senior management.

Criteria for re-assessment **31** Re-assessment will be necessary if there are changes in the operation, plant or buildings. It may also be necessary to re-assess after particular fires; or after other incidents which give rise to a risk of fire; or where the results of monitoring reveal previously unforeseen inadequacies in the control measures or greater than anticipated hazard/risk.

HOUSEKEEPING

32 It is essential that mills have a culture of good housekeeping to prevent hazards from waste materials lying around. The following actions are recommended:

(a) Wherever possible, trim and/or waste should be automatically removed;

(b) A programme of regular cleaning and waste removal needs to be set up. This needs to be done frequently enough to prevent any build-up of broke, dust or other waste;

(c) Papermaking machines should be cleaned regularly by the machine crew or a special hygiene crew;

(d) Clearing away of broke etc from the paper machine should be a normal part of planned shuts. Whenever there are unplanned shuts the opportunity should be taken to remove broke etc which cannot be removed with the machine running;

(e) Cleaning must be thorough and include office and storage areas;

(f) Particular attention should be paid to those areas where broke paper, dust or trim is produced, as this is easily ignited. Dust will accumulate on ledges and beams, and this should be regularly removed with vacuum equipment.

33 Contractors may produce significant amounts of combustible waste. There should be a system to ensure that this is removed promptly.

....

34 A sufficient number of non-combustible waste containers should be provided at appropriate points. There should be an organised system for the prompt removal of the large volumes of waste liable to be generated at both paper-making and reeling and slitting machines.

35 Chemicals should only be in the workplace while actually in use. Used containers must be disposed of safely or returned to a suitable storage area.

36 Attention should be paid to housekeeping in other areas, eg engineers' stores where packaging material needs to be promptly and safely removed.

SMOKING

37 Each mill should have a policy for controlling smoking. Workpeople need to be consulted when this policy is drawn up. Once non-smoking areas have been established, the policy should be strictly enforced. In general, smoking should only be allowed in designated, safe areas.

VANDALISM AND INTRUDERS

38 Fires started by vandals or intruders have been a serious problem at paper mills, especially where sites are large and there are extensive external stocks of paper bales or reels. Adequate security should be provided to reduce the chance of intruders entering the mill. The following measures should be considered:

(a) The site perimeter may need a wall or fence at least 2 m high which is regularly inspected and maintained in good condition;

(b) Stocks of paper etc should not be kept up against or near site boundaries;

(c) There should be sufficient lighting in storage areas so that security staff can easily check for intruders.

(d) Access points to the site should be limited and these should be manned to check visitors coming onto the site;

(e) Limiting the means of access should not be at the expense of restricting the ability of personnel to escape from fires or the ease with which fire fighting can be carried out;

(f) High-risk areas, eg boundaries, storage areas or parts of the site which are rarely visited by mill personnel should be continuously monitored by means of a closed circuit television system.

39 Detailed advice about security can be obtained from your local police force or from your insurance company.

SAFETY OF MILL FIRE TEAMS

40   Many mills, especially those which are large or remote from local authority fire stations, have their own 'mill fire teams'. These can perform a valuable service in preventing small fires from spreading and giving detailed advice about the premises to local authority fire-fighters. However, such teams must not be put into a situation or put themselves into a situation which is outside their competence. Some mills may have occupational fire brigades. Running of these is a specialised matter and the local authority fire brigade should be consulted. Guidance is given in the Loss Prevention Council *Code of practice - occupational fire brigades* (Reference 3). 'Mill fire teams' means a group of employees trained to implement fire safety plans to save lives and take initial action to protect property by utilising first-aid fire-fighting equipment. An 'occupational fire brigade' is an organised body wholly funded by a body other than a statutory fire authority. It is maintained for the purposes of saving life and protecting property in the event of fire or other emergency in locations owned, managed or occupied by the sponsor.

41   The following points should be considered:

(a)   The role of a mill fire team should be clearly defined. Management, fire teams and safety representatives should be in no doubt as to the level of physical fitness, training, equipment and competence expected of the team;

(b)   The local authority fire brigade should be consulted about the procedures to be followed in case of fire. Management must issue clear instructions including specifying personnel to make decisions at as early a stage as possible. The limits of the mill fire team's responsibilities before calling outside assistance should be made clear. Where there is the slightest doubt of the ability of the mill fire team to cope with the situation then the local authority fire brigade should be called. In many mills it would be appropriate for the local fire authority brigade to be called irrespective of the size of the incident and the mill fire team to confine itself to first-aid fire-fighting that it can then carry out safely;

(c)   Appropriate training should be given to the mill fire teams. It will not be enough for only initial basic training to be given. It is more likely that training will be a continuous process. Mills are advised to contact the local authority brigade as they may well be able to provide training facilities. Particular points which should be covered include:

   (i)   causes of fires in paper mills and associated premises, ie offices, stores etc;

   (ii)   basic fire-fighting techniques;

   (iii)   past experience of fires in the paper industry;

(iv) behaviour of fires;

(v) use, location and limitations of all relevant equipment;

(vi) procedures in case of fire;

(vii) familiarisation with all parts of the mill site including location of both static and mains water supplies;

(viii) limitations on what team members are expected to do;

(ix) communications with each other in a fire situation;

(x) liaison, training and exercising with the local authority brigade;

(xi) basic first aid;

(xii) behaviour of personnel in fire situations; and

(xiii) observing fire drills.

(d) Suitable equipment should be provided, which is appropriate for the level at which the mill fire team is expected to operate. Equipment needs to be properly maintained by competent staff;

(e) Breathing apparatus which is provided for other purposes should not be used for fire-fighting unless it is by an occupational fire brigade who are appropriately trained and use proper local authority fire brigade breathing apparatus control procedures;

(f) There needs to be a clear and effective chain of command for the mill fire team. In a fire the safety of the fire-fighters depends on there being no confusion about who is in charge;

(g) On arrival, the senior officer of the local authority fire brigade has the sole charge and control of all operations for the extinction of the fire (see Appendix 2, paragraph 22);

(h) The procedures for liaison with the local authority brigade need to be worked out in consultation with them. On arrival of the local authority fire brigade and following consultation between the appropriate manager and fire officer in charge, the mill fire team may be requested to withdraw partly or wholly from the fire incident. They may however be asked to provide advice and assistance to the local fire authority fire brigade in relation to the premises and processes;

(i) Senior management should report on incidents, including the way in which these were tackled, and monitor the mill fire team;

(j)   There should be adequate and suitable insurance cover for the mill fire teams.

HAZARDS AND PRECAUTIONS IN VARIOUS OPERATIONS

Storage   **42**   The main principles of safe storage are to segregate the storage areas from the process work areas, and to segregate combustible materials from each other so that in the event of a fire in one area, other areas are not affected. Only authorised people should be allowed access to fire-separated storage areas.

43   One method of reducing the risk of fire spread and controlling the fire size is to ensure that the fire is vented in its early stages. This may be achieved preferably by automatic smoke venting or the provision of roof panels which will fail early in any fire. Such provisions have the added advantage of allowing fire fighters to enter the building and locate the seat of the fire.

44   Storage in a separate building, a single-storey extension to the main building, or in a safe place in the open air is preferable, but this may not always be possible. In these cases storage areas should be separated from workrooms by partitioning with a fire resistance of not less than half an hour for personal protection. Higher standards of fire resistance will be required for protection of the building and contents. If frequent access is needed into a store automatically closing fire doors will provide a satisfactory standard of protection. The risk of fire spreading is reduced by compartmentalisation of storage areas.

45   In certain limited cases where storage areas cannot be separated, safety will need to be achieved by other means (but see paragraph 113). This will require an assessment of the characteristics and quantity of material stored, conditions of use and storage, the nature of the building and the adequacy of emergency procedures and fire precautions. For example, it may be possible to achieve safety by a combination of other measures such as spatial separation, fire or smoke detectors linked to an alarm system, sprinklers and smoke control systems. Although such arrangements may be reasonable to protect employees, it must be remembered that lack of physical separation can lead to more extensive fire damage.

46   Separation may be specified in a fire certificate or by the conditions of a petroleum licence. Separation may also be required where the Highly Flammable Liquids and Liquefied Petroleum Gases Regulations 1972 apply.

47   The following points are particularly worth noting:

(a)   Gangways in stacking areas should be sufficiently wide to ensure free movement to fire exits; a currently accepted minimum figure is 1.1 m. Where mechanically powered or hand trucks are used in the gangway it

. . . .

Page 13 Paper and Board Industry Advisory Committee

should be wide enough for people to pass freely. Gangways should also be clearly marked, for example by lines marked on the floor, and kept clear. An exit should be provided from each end of any main gangway and dead ends should be avoided;

(b) Stored combustible material should be kept well away from potential sources of ignition, such as light fittings and direct fired or convector type heaters. Raw materials and products should be stored so that they do not obstruct means of escape, fire-alarm call points, fire-detection equipment, fire-fighting equipment or fire doors and shutters and in particular should be kept well away from sprinkler heads;

(c) Smoking should be prohibited in the store;

(d) Boilers, emergency generators and other similar plant should be segregated by fire resisting walls, floors and doors;

(e) Battery charging should not be done in storage areas;

(f) Used pallets and empty containers stored outside should be well away from openings into buildings and preferably at least 1 m clear of any boundary fence;

(g) Vigilance against vandalism and intruders is needed, especially where there are very large quantities of stock and few employees;

(h) Guidance on the storage of packaged dangerous substances can be found in Reference 4;

(i) Apart from paper there may be other flammable solids, eg foam plastic. These should be stored safely. Information is given in Reference 5.

(j) Stocks of paper should not be kept up against or near site boundaries or against the walls of buildings.

Reel storage

48 Storage of paper reels can create particular fire hazards. Management should assess the risk arising from such storage and see that the necessary safeguards and controls are applied, taking account of information provided by the suppliers. Information on the storage of paper reels in buildings provided with automatic sprinklers including the height of stacks is given in Reference 6.

49 The most likely material to be ignited is loose paper material, eg discarded wrappers, loose ends, and loose paper on damaged reels. These problems need to be identified at an early stage. Damaged reels should be wrapped or taped on delivery.

50 Where reels are stacked vertically in columns there will inevitably be gaps between the columns. In the event of a fire starting at the bottom of the stack the gap will constitute a chimney. Rapid burning will follow as air drawn in at the bottom will accelerate up the chimney, typically to a speed of approximately 15 metres per second. The rate of burning increases rapidly with increasing stack height. This rapid vertical flame spread is compounded by rapid horizontal spread when the layers of paper begin to unwind. This type of fire may be difficult or impossible to control with conventional sprinklers. The risk of rapid fire is therefore reduced if reels are not stacked on end.

51 The following special precautions are required in reel storage areas:

(a) Floors need to be kept clean and free of loose paper. Other combustible material should not be kept in the reel store;

(b) Damaged reels should be repaired by taping or rewrapping;

(c) Where reels are stacked vertically the spaces between the reels should be as small as possible (less than 100 mm). This should help prevent the peeling off process that accelerates fire-spread. If spaces are less than 25 mm the flow is likely to be throttled and the rate of fire spread further reduced. Alternatively spaces should be wide enough (more than 1.1 m) to allow normal access. Figure 2 shows two stacking arrangements. The arrangement in Figure 2(b) is preferable as the voids between reels are smaller and less well ventilated. Care should however be taken to ensure that reels can be removed without disturbing adjacent stacks.

(d) Vertically stacked, banded reels in purpose-built separate buildings with proper fire separation, venting and restricted access may be stacked as high as can be safely achieved with the stacking equipment. Information and advice will be required from the fire authority and insurers on fire detection, protection and extinguishing systems, dependant on the stacking height but especially if stacks are greater than 7.2 m high (see Reference 7);

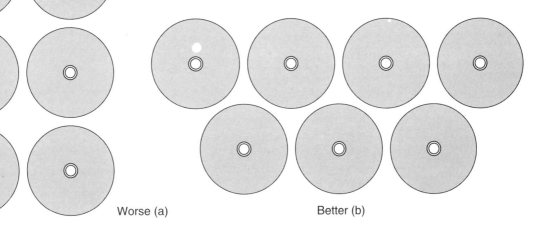

Worse (a) Better (b)

Figure 2 Patterns of vertical reel stacking. In (b) gaps between reels have been minimised so reducing the chimney effect in the case of fire

(e) Smoke venting etc (see paragraph 43);

(f) Frequent inspection and checks by supervision.

52 Stacked reels can present an unacceptable risk to people in inner rooms such as offices, storerooms, toilets etc. The presence of stacked reels in the vicinity of the only escape route from these rooms raises the outer room (ie store) to high-risk status. Unless reels are sufficiently remote from the escape route from any inner room, then the inner room should have an alternative exit either direct to open air or via a separate fire-resisting compartment.

53 The stacking of reels can have an adverse effect on the audibility of the fire alarm system. If stacking is introduced into an area not previously used for that purpose or if there is any material increase in stacking, a check should be made to ensure that the alarm is still audible throughout the whole of the premises.

Bale storage - general

54 Bales of paper, especially waste, present a high fire risk, as loose material is always present. Bales should be neatly stacked. Stacks should be limited in size to reduce the fire loading and laid out in straight rows with adequate gangways between stacks which allow easy access for fire-fighting.

55 Gangways should be as wide as possible to prevent fire-spread through radiated heat. Housekeeping should be to a high standard with regular sweeping-up to prevent loose paper accumulating. Gangways should be kept clear of all debris of material which could impede escape or hinder fire-fighting.

56 Local authority legislation may limit the size of stacks, and mills are advised to check with them.

57 In all normal circumstances the system of work should not permit pedestrians to enter bale storage areas.

58 Stacks that are not protected by a fire detection and alarm system should be checked regularly by suitably trained staff.

59 Sources of ignition should be kept away from stacks.

60 An adequate water supply must be available in the event of a fire, if effective fire-fighting is to be undertaken.

Indoor storage

61 Fire in baled paper is difficult to extinguish and generates heavy smoke. In large storage areas automatic venting of smoke is desirable to facilitate fire-fighting operations and to reduce structural and stock damage. As a rule of

thumb 1 m2 of openable ventilation to 50 m² of storage is reasonable, **but it is advisable to seek specialist advice.**

62   Keeping piles as narrow as practical, consistent with the configuration of the building, is good practice. Adequate main aisles (generally not less than 3 m) and cross aisles are necessary to provide means of access, as well as access for fire-fighting. Aisles should be free of obstructions (eg fork-lift trucks) when the building is not in use.

63   Bales should ideally be protected by a sprinkler system, suitably designed to cope with the height of the bales. Bales should have a maximum height of 5 m and in all cases should be 3 m below the level of the sprinklers.

Outdoor storage

64   Stacks should not exceed 7 m in height.

65   Stacks should be separated from one another by gangways at least three times the height of the highest adjacent stack, with a minimum of 6 m between stacks. It should be noted that providing the separation distances suggested will not necessarily prevent fire spreading from pile to pile, but the rate of spread will be reduced and, with time, the chances of early control increased.

Storage of gases

66   Gases in cylinders can be flammable, toxic, corrosive or inert. Even cylinders of inert gases pose a hazard in a fire as they can become over pressurised and rupture violently.

67   All gas cylinders should be stored away from flammable liquids, combustible materials, corrosives and toxic materials. Cylinders containing gases of differing hazard, eg toxic, flammable, corrosive and oxidizing (including oxygen) should be stored separately from one another. The main points of note are:

(a)   Gas cylinders should preferably be stored in the open air in a lockable wire mesh cage for security. For details of separation distances from buildings and boundaries see References 8, 9 and 10;

(b)   Except for small quantities, cylinders of liquefied petroleum gas, eg propane and butane should be kept separately from other gases (Reference 8);

(c)   If flammable gases are to be used in a building, the preferred arrangement is for the cylinders to be kept in the open air and piped into the workroom by permanent fixed metal pipework at as low a pressure as is possible.

(d)   Bulk tanks of Liquefied Petroleum Gas should be installed in accordance with *Storage of LPG at fixed installations* (Reference 11).

Storage of wood and wood-chips

68 Some mills have stocks of wood and/or wood-chips. These should be stored separately from other materials. Stacks of wood should have good access for fire-fighting purposes. Wood-chips could smoulder for some time if they have been on fire in the chipper or could spontaneously ignite if left for long periods in the open air. Piles of wood-chips should be used in rotation and cleared so that the chips cannot stand for long periods of time. Duct work and silos for wood-chips will contain dust. They should be fitted with fire detection/suppression systems and, as appropriate, with adequate explosion relief panels.

Paper dust

69 Paper dust presents a very high risk of fire and may under certain conditions be explosible. Although the problems are likely to be more extensive in tissue mills, all paper mills, especially if there are paper/dust collectors, could be hazardous. Flammable dusts are liable to explode if they are in a finely divided state and become airborne in a cloud. Paper dust is generated wherever certain processes are carried out, eg webs going over rollers, or being slit or cut, or sheets hitting stops. It is preferable for dust to be collected as near to its source as practicable. Local exhaust ventilation (LEV) equipment should be provided wherever substantial quantities of dust are created.

70 LEV equipment should be designed to collect as much dust as practicable and remove it to a safe place. Duct work should be made of fire-resistant material. It is preferable for dust collectors to be sited outside buildings and they should be fitted with adequate explosion relief. Guidance on such systems is given in the Institute of Chemical Engineers' *Guide to dust explosion, prevention and protection* (Reference 12). It may be appropriate to fit suitable fire/explosion suppression equipment. The design is highly specialised and advice should be taken from a competent supplier or consultant.

71 General housekeeping in areas where dust can settle needs to be of a very high order. Substantial quantities of dust should never be allowed to accumulate and regular cleaning will be needed to achieve this. Cleaning of paper dust should be done with a vacuum cleaner except where it is not physically possible to do so (for example if it has coagulated). Air lines may be used for removing coagulated material as long as any loose dust has already been removed by vacuuming.

Fires in machine hoods

72 Fires in machine hoods pose risks to those needing to be inside as well as to the plant and surrounding structures. Access within the hood must be designed to facilitate emergency escape, and procedures in place so that when the hood is down and the machine is running, only the crew is permitted access. All other access must be authorised by local supervision. Specialist advice, including that of the local fire brigade and the company insurers, will be needed for the design of smoke and heat venting systems. Similarly for existing hoods consideration can be given to opportunities which may exist for controlling a fire or ameliorating its effects by use of any air circulation or venting systems or other controls. The advice should extend to whether the machine should be stopped or kept running in the event of fire. The procedure should also indicate when the decision to evacuate overrides the machine condition so that crews are not put at risk. An example of one mill's arrangements is given in Appendix 6.

Starch 73 Many mills have bulk starch handling facilities often with large silos for storage. Starch presents an explosion hazard and the following precautions should be taken:

(a) Storage silos should be provided with adequate explosion relief panels (see Reference 12) and earthed in accordance with BS 7430: 1965 (Reference 13);

(b) The silo should preferably be fitted with fixed lighting, suitable for use in explosible dust, to remove the need to introduce temporary lighting (Reference 14). If temporary lighting has to be used it should be protected to a suitable standard;

(c) Pipes should either be able to contain an internal explosion or be able to vent any explosion safely;

(d) The transfer system should be electrically bonded throughout its length. In particular, earthing straps should be provided across points of discontinuity such as a sight glass or a section of plastic pipe;

(e) If any hose or pipe is made of insulating material incorporating metal reinforcement on the inside surface, the reinforcement should be electrically bonded to the end couplings;

(f) Where possible metal pipe couplings should be used;

(g) At the transfer point, the delivery vehicle must be electrically bonded to the receiving installation, preferably by using hoses of all metal construction or low electrical resistance material;

(h) Any non-return valve fitted on the vehicle downstream of the air compressor should be inspected regularly for effective operation. Where reasonably practicable such a valve should be fitted;

(i) Combustible foam or wadding should not be used inside silencers fitted on the outlets of vehicle air compressors;

(j) To avoid the back flow of powder the operating instructions for tanker discharge should clearly indicate that before the compressor is turned off, all vents in the downstream system should be opened, for long enough to depressurise the tank and discharge equipment. Alternatively, positive isolation of the air supply downstream of the compressor should be specified. In this case protection of the compressor to prevent overheating while working against a closed pipe is likely to be needed. Items (h)-(j) will be the responsibility of the tanker operators.

74 A likely cause of explosions is maintenance or repair work involving hot work (eg burning, welding or grinding). For precautions see paragraphs 94 to 97.

Hydrogen sulphide

75 Although hydrogen sulphide is primarily a toxic hazard there have been a number of explosions in chests and tanks during shuts in foreign mills. It has been found that hydrogen and hydrogen sulphide (both flammable gases) generation results from an aerobic bacterial action on paper fibre or other organic material. The necessary growth conditions are undisturbed organic material in a warm aqueous system at a near-neutral or slightly alkaline pH. These conditions are increasingly likely to occur during mill shuts where neutral or alkaline papermaking conditions apply. Note that if hydrogen formation occurs in stagnant conditions, it may remain attached to paper fibres until agitation is recommenced; hydrogen could then be released into the air.

76 It is preferable at the start of mill-shuts or other sustained breaks in production (eg a weekend) to empty and clean thoroughly all chests and white water storage.

77 If there is provision for agitation of the stock the following options may be considered if there are exceptional reasons to do so:

(a) Continue agitation to prevent aerobic conditions and maintain an adequate level of biocide; or

(b) Add sufficient biocide, agitate fully and allow to stand. Consult the biocide supplier to determine how much and how often biocide should be added to give adequate protection;

(c) In either case ensure that the chest or tank is adequately ventilated, so that any traces of flammable gases are dissipated;

(d) In addition, tests must be carried out to confirm the absence of hydrogen and hydrogen sulphide before hot work is permitted nearby or on the chests etc, or if there is any ignition sources in the locality;

(e) Tanks should be cleaned regularly. Even if there is ample agitation of stock, debris can remain undisturbed, allowing bacteria to breed;

(f) For any entry to chests and tanks a confined space permit-to-work must be issued.

78 Note that hydrogen sulphide can also be generated in effluent plants and appropriate precautions should be taken to prevent risk (see *Entry into confined spaces*, Reference 15).

Charging of electrically operated lift trucks

79 The following points need to be considered:

(a) If a metal tool or other electrically conducting object short-circuits the terminals of a cell or cells it will become hot and may cause burns. In addition sparks and molten metal may be ejected. Insulated tools should always be used and, before working on a battery, people should remove any metallic items from hands, wrist and neck, together with any metallic items that may fall from their pockets.

(b) Hydrogen and oxygen gases are emitted from a battery when it is being charged. Hydrogen/air mixtures produce violent explosions if ignited and it has to be assumed that this mixture is present in the immediate vicinity of the cell tops at all times. To minimise the risk of explosion:

   (i)   charging should be carried out in an area used only for that purpose which is not near any combustible materials (see also paragraph 47(e));

   (ii) the charging area should have good natural high level ventilation immediately above the batteries (see Reference 16);

   (iii) light fittings should be of a totally enclosed industrial type, eg bulkhead fittings and preferably positioned other than directly above the charging area;

   (iv) smoking or naked lights should be prohibited in the area. Appropriate notices should be displayed;

   (v)   anything capable of causing a spark should not be used in the vicinity of the cell tops;

   (vi) a proper plug and socket arrangement should normally be used for routinely connecting the charger to the batteries - the charger should be switched off before making or breaking the connection;

   (vii) battery covers may be open or removed during charging but all vent plugs should be in position;

   (viii) when carrying out maintenance on the battery all electrical circuits including the charger should be switched off before making or breaking connections at the battery terminals. The lead connected to the vehicle framework should always be disconnected first and reconnected last;

(c) Appropriate fire-fighting equipment should be readily available (see Appendix 3).

Flammable liquids

General

80 The Highly Flammable Liquids and Liquefied Petroleum Gases Regulations 1972 apply to those liquids having a flashpoint of less than 32°C and which support combustion, ie at ambient temperature they give off vapours that are easily ignited by, for example, a small spark or hot surfaces; in some cases the Petroleum (Consolidation) Act and the Petroleum (Mixtures) Order will apply. The flashpoint should be given in the suppliers health and safety data sheet. The detailed advice on storage of flammable liquids given in References 17, 18 and 19 should be followed (certain variations for liquids with flashpoints in the range 32-55°C are given in the documents).

81 The main hazard in the storage of flammable liquids is fire involving either the bulk liquid or escaping liquid or vapour; the vapours are usually heavier than air and can travel long distances so that any major spillage will almost inevitably reach a source of ignition. Such incidents may be caused by inadequacies in design, manufacture, installation, maintenance, or by equipment failure or maloperation, together with exposure to a nearby source of ignition. Ignition of the vapours from flammable liquids remains a possibility until the vapour concentration is reduced below the lower flammable limit. The lower flammable limit of a material is the concentration (usually expressed as the percentage, by volume, of the material mixed with air) below which the mixture is too lean to undergo combustion; this varies with different materials but it is usually about 1.5% in air.

Use

82 Guidance is available in Reference 20 on the use of flammable liquids. The following general points apply wherever flammable liquids are used or kept:

(a) Stocks of flammable liquids and empty or part-used containers should be properly stored (see References 17, 18 and 19). Except when actually in use containers should be kept closed in an appropriate secure and properly bunded storage area;

(b) The quantity of flammable liquids in workrooms should be kept to a minimum, normally to no more than a half-day's supply;

(c) Flammable liquids should be conveyed and handled in enclosed systems where possible, for example by piping supplies from the storage location to the point of use; where a connection is frequently broken and remade, a sealed-end coupling is preferred. Containers should be kept covered. Proprietary safety containers with self-closing lids and caps should be used where possible for dispensing and applying small quantities of flammable liquids. The lids and caps of containers should be replaced after use. No container should be opened in such a way (for example by punching a hole or cutting off the top) that it cannot be safely reclosed;

(d)   The store should be used exclusively for the storage of flammable liquids and should not normally be used for dispensing;

(e)   Rags impregnated with flammable solvents should be kept in metal bins with well-fitting, preferably self-closing lids and removed from the workroom each shift;

(f)   Sources of ignition should be controlled (eg see References 21 and 22);

(g)   Flammable liquids should be stored and handled in well-ventilated conditions. In some cases it may be necessary to use exhaust ventilation to control flammable vapour;

83   One of the major uses of flammable liquids in the paper industry is the coating or laminating processes. Guidance on some particular hazards and precautions is given in Appendix 7.

Electricity   **84**   Electricity can cause fires or explosions in a number of ways. The principal mechanisms causing fire are:

(a)   overheating of cables and electrical equipment due to overloading of conductors;

(b)   leakage currents due to damaged or inadequate insulation;

(c)   overheating of flammable materials placed too close to electrical equipment which is otherwise operating normally (eg equipment covered in flammable dust);

(d)   The ignition of flammable materials by arcing or sparking of electrical equipment.

85   Explosions can occur in switchgear, motors or power cables if they are subjected to excessive currents or suffer prolonged internal arcing faults.

86   Electrical systems should be designed and constructed and maintained to prevent danger. The Institution of Electrical Engineers Wiring Regulations give much practical guidance for systems up to 1000V. There are many British Standards which give information on how electrical equipment can be safely constructed and maintained. It is important that electrical systems should be adequately rated for the job they have to do.

87   It is essential that competent people are used for installation and maintenance of electrical equipment.

88   If the ignition of flammable materials is to be prevented then there should be good housekeeping standards.

89 Guidance on the Electricity Regulations is given in the Memorandum of guidance on the Electricity at Work Regulations 1989 (Reference 23).

Maintenance of plant

90 Plant which is poorly maintained is a cause of fires. In a survey carried out by one local authority fire brigade 60 per cent of all fires were due to poor maintenance of plant or premises. It is usually a combination of circumstances which leads to fires. Typically circumstances which contribute to the start of fires are:

(a) poor housekeeping, eg build-up of dust or paper, causing overheating (see paragraphs 32-36);

(b) lack of bearing lubrication. Especially where there are many bearings it is easy for some to be overlooked, leading to frictional heating;

(c) friction heating (eg due to drive belts rubbing);

(d) electrical malfunction (see paragraphs 84-86);

(e) flammable materials used in contact with hot surfaces (eg lagging materials not properly separated from steam pipe flanges) (see Reference 25);

(f) leaking of flammable liquids or gases from valves or flanges (note that in elevated temperatures most oils and greases will burn vigorously);

(g) static sparks (eg from inadequate earthing of solvent tanks).

91 There may need to be a formal planned maintenance programme to ensure plant is properly maintained. If instrumentation is used to monitor the condition of the machine, the information gained (eg bearing temperatures) may be of use in reducing the chances of fire.

Engineering and construction work

92 Engineering and construction operations can significantly increase the risk of fire. Extra precautions are needed to control processes such as welding and cutting, and where there are likely to be people such as contractors who are unfamiliar with the site, systems of work or hazards. Guidance on hot work is given in paragraphs 94-97.

93 There needs to be an assessment of engineering and construction operations so that the range of hazards is identified and plans made to control them. These hazards will include the risks of materials used in the work which are stored on site during the work. Methods of work and storage facilities, including those for contractors, need to be clearly specified and monitored, especially if contractors are bringing equipment or flammable materials onto site. There should be control of fire hazards introduced by contractors and provision made for the storage and disposal of waste materials. Temporary storage areas for flammable liquids and gases should be set up in safe places. Management need to oversee the work to ensure the risk of fire is minimised.

Hot work

94 Certain activities, eg the use of welding, flame cutting blow-lamps or portable grinding equipment in areas where paper or flammable liquids are stored or used, need to be strictly controlled. This must be done through a written permit to work for the people involved. This should apply both to in-house and contractors staff.

95 Any employees and outside contractors who are to take part in such activities should be left in no doubt that work may not begin until the person who is to issue the permit has explained fully the safety precautions that must be observed. It is imperative that a written handover procedure is adopted. Appendix 4 gives details of the principles to be applied (see also Reference 27).

96 The permit should include details of:

(a) preliminary measures to ensure the area is free from combustible materials;

(b) the fire-fighting equipment which should be at the site of the work;

(c) the supervision needed; and

(d) the measures which are required on the completion of the work, and for checking that an incipient fire cannot break out at a later time.

97 Fuel gas and oxygen cylinders should not be taken into a confined space unless this is unavoidable because of the risk of leakage. All cylinders, hoses and torches should be removed from a confined space on completion of work and when there is any substantial break in the work activity, eg more than half an hour.

GENERAL FIRE PRECAUTIONS

98 The role of general fire precautions in the management of fire risk and need for written emergency arrangements are introduced in paragraph 23. Their application in detail is set out below.

99 Most paper and board mills will require a fire certificate because of the numbers of people employed and presence of highly flammable materials. If material changes have taken place since the certificate was issued then a new or amended certificate will be required. Application should be made to the fire authority. The fire certificate sets out minimum standards of precautions in case of fire so that people inside the mill are able to go to a safe place if a fire occurs. If significant changes are planned then prior consultation with the fire authority is required (see Appendix 2). The local authority should also be consulted to determine whether building regulations approval is needed.

| **Means of escape** | **100** In all premises there must be means of escape appropriate to the risk. All means of escape provided should be kept unobstructed and available for use for the whole of the time that the premises are occupied. It should be possible to open doors easily and immediately from the inside without the use of a key. |

101 Circumstances in premises will vary, but the principle to be applied is that a person should be able to turn away from a fire and reach a place of safety, in the open air, within a reasonable distance and without outside assistance. Arrangements for people with disabilities should be carefully considered.

102 Officers of the local authority fire brigade consider the following when assessing the means of escape (detailed information on these is given in the relevant Scottish Home Department's guidance documents (see References 1 and 29 and Appendix 2):

(a) fire hazards and fire risks in the premises;

(b) the indication of exits and escape routes;

(c) the protection of escape routes;

(d) construction of the building;

(e) occupancy of the building;

(f) number of exits available;

(g) number of people involved;

(h) travel distances to a place of safety (these are prescribed for particular circumstances);

(i) provision of emergency lighting.

103 Pending the issue of a fire certificate the existing means of escape should be maintained so that they can be safely used, eg free from obstruction, doors capable of being easily and immediately opened without the use of a key (for further information see Reference 30).

Fire alarms **104** A fire alarm gives early warning of the outbreak of fire so that people can leave buildings before the fire endangers them and reach a place of safety. Modern systems can operate in a variety of modes. In some cases it is not necessary to evacuate the whole of a premise if only part is affected and fire cannot spread. Some sites have a two-stage system where occupants not immediately at risk are alerted to a fire but not immediately evacuated. The provision of these systems requires expertise, and the local authority fire safety officer must be consulted.

105 A fire alarm system will normally be required in all paper mills.

106 A type M system (manually operated electrical fire warning) as described in British Standard 5839: Part 1: 1988 (Reference 30) will generally be considered as the minimum statutory requirement for premises requiring a fire certificate. Among the matters to be determined are the provision and siting of call points, the siting of alarm sounders and of control and indicating equipment. If alterations to plant or buildings are made, the audibility of the alarm should be checked. Alarm systems should take account of the problems involved in noisy environments, especially where hearing protection is being worn. Consideration may need to be given to using visual indications as well as audible alarms. Fire alarms will need to be tested regularly. Fire certificates will generally specify the tests which should be carried out.

107 Automatic fire detection (eg smoke and/or heat detectors) is desirable as a means of protecting the property by ensuring early warning of any fire. Where manual and automatic systems are installed in the same building, they should be incorporated in a single system (Reference 30). However, it is only likely to become a requirement under the terms of a fire certificate where the fire risk assessment indicates that the premises or part of the premises are of high fire risk.

Training

108 In order to minimise the risk to people in case of fire, it is essential that they all receive adequate fire safety training appropriate to their role. Fire safety training can be broadly divided into four types:

(a) *Induction training* should be given to all new staff (including contractors) before they start work and should include an explanation of evacuation procedures, method of raising the alarm and any rules concerning smoking. They should be made familiar with the escape routes from any place where they have to work to specified assembly points. This could be done by walking along the routes or by adequate signs and written information.

(b) *Basic and refresher training* should be given to all staff, preferably at least twice a year, but at least once a year. The training should cover the following points:

(i) The action to be taken on discovering fire;

(ii) The action to take on hearing the fire alarm including evacuation and roll call procedures;

(iii) The location of fire alarm call points and how to raise the alarm;

(iv) How the fire brigade is called (unless this is to be done only by designated staff);

(v)   The location and use of fire equipment and the dangers of using the wrong type of extinguisher;

(vi)   Knowledge of escape routes including the operation of any special emergency door fastenings and any stairway not in regular use;

(vii)   Location and identification of fire doors and their importance in restricting fire spread and protecting escape routes;

(viii) Stopping machines and processes and isolating power supplies where appropriate (each mill needs to draw up its own procedures - see Appendix 6 for an example from one mill). Personal protection must be paramount;

(ix)   Warning against stopping to collect belongings or re-entering buildings.

(c)   *Training of key personnel* should apply to certain categories of staff. Every person identified in the emergency plan as a person responsible for supervising and controlling the putting into effect of the plan and the conduct of fire drills should have access to the risk assessments and to the emergency plan. They should also be given additional instruction in matters which will be their particular responsibilities over the above basic training. Specific aspects of training will include the supervision of evacuation and roll-call procedures, the control of contractors and the safety of visitors in the event of fire and liaison with the local authority fire brigade. These key personnel need to be clear how they fit into the overall emergency plan. Key personnel covered by this section will include:

(i)   heads of departments;

(ii)   engineering and maintenance staff;

(iii)   boiler house crews;

(iv)   supervisors;

(v)   security staff;

(vi)   mill fire teams;

(vii)   wardens/marshals;

(viii) safety representatives;

(ix)   telephonists;

(x)   tour guides.

(d) Key personnel should receive refresher training at appropriate intervals;

(e) Mill fire teams are likely to need a continuous programme of training to ensure they are, and remain competent to carry out their duties.

109 Changes in procedures, any new hazards or any lessons learned from fire incidents or drills should be taken into account in refresher training.

110 A practice fire drill should be carried out twice a year. It is a good exercise to simulate conditions in which one or more exits or escape routes from the building are obstructed. During these drills the fire alarm should be operated by a member of staff, who is told of a supposed outbreak of fire. The fire routine should then be followed as fully as circumstances permit. The special needs of employees who have disabilities and/or sensory impairments should receive particular attention. The practice fire drill should be part of management's consideration and scrutiny of the quality of training.

111 Records should be kept of the maintenance done to ensure that means of escape, fire-fighting equipment, fire detection and warning equipment remain in efficient working order. They should also be kept of the instruction and training provided and specifically of every fire drill. All training and drills should be based on written instructions and be recorded in a log book. The records should include:

(a) the date of the training or drill;

(b) duration of training;

(c) fire drill evacuation times;

(d) name of person giving instruction;

(e) names of people receiving instructions;

(f) the nature of the instruction or drill;

(g) any observations/remedial action.

112 Printed fire instruction notices should be displayed at conspicuous positions in the building stating in concise terms what staff and others should do if a fire is discovered or if they hear the alarm. The notices should be permanently fixed in position and suitably protected to prevent loss or defacement. The fire certificate will normally specify the content of the notice.

Automatic sprinklers and automatic smoke control systems

113 For complex or high fire-risk premises, a greater emphasis is now being given to a range of specialised protection measures. These include automatic fire detection techniques, life safety sprinkler systems, smoke management, as well as passive fire defence such as compartmentalisation and the fire resistance elements of structure. A total fire defence package will, in addition to providing the life safety measures to satisfy legislation, afford a high level of property protection.

114 Installation of such systems is usually a specialist job and mills should seek advice from the local authority fire safety officer, their insurers, and firms having the appropriate expertise. If sections of such systems are closed down, the fire risk may be increased. There should be consultation with both the local authority fire brigade and the insurers.

Gas flooding fire extinguishing systems

115 These may be used to protect certain processes, eg computer suites and data stores from fire. Exposure to the extinguishing agents (carbon dioxide, nitrogen, or in newer installations halon) may be hazardous in the event of accidental discharge. Exposure to the agent and products of combustion during discharge in a fire may also be hazardous. Some systems may be local, only protecting individual machines and not presenting a hazard to individuals. Others flood larger areas, and personnel need to be protected against asphyxiation or the effect of toxic fumes.

116 Suitable safeguards should be incorporated where there is a need to protect personnel. Such systems should be under manual control when people are present and could be affected. Warning signs should be provided and in the case of a total flooding system there should be an indicator showing whether the system is on manual or automatic. Adequate means of escape should be provided and maintained. The system itself should be well maintained. Further guidance is available in Reference 31.

Extinguishers and hose reels

117 All premises should be provided with means for fighting fire. The aim is to provide people with the means of extinguishing small fires in their early stages. They are only of use for first-aid fire-fighting. The location of such equipment should be identified in accordance with BS5499 Parts 1 and 3 (Reference 26).

118 In selecting appropriate means for fighting fire the nature of the materials likely to be found should be considered. Different types of fire are defined in BS EN 2 *Classification of fires* (Reference 32). These and the appropriate extinguishing agents are described in Appendix 3.

119 People on the premises should be aware of the dangers and limitations of fighting a fire with fire extinguishers.

120 The fire certificate issued under the Fire Precautions Act 1971 will specify minimum life safety requirements; employers may wish to make additional provision (in consultation with their insurers) for the protection of property.

Access for fire appliances and assistance to the fire brigade

121 There needs to be a good means of access both into the mill and to all parts of the mill site for fire appliances. The local fire brigade should be consulted for minimum sizes of entrances and roadways etc. For new or altered premises these distances are now set out in Approved Document B5 to the Building Regulations (see Reference 33). Information which will be of help to the local authority fire brigade should be readily available at the entrance to the site (eg site plan, location of water supplies, main plant isolation points, COSHH register).

122 There also need to be adequate water supplies for the fire brigade to use. Hydrants need to be sited and identified so that fire-fighters can easily reach any part of the mill site with adequate supplies of water. They should be so sited that fire-fighters are not likely to be at risk from a fire while using them. Regular tests should be carried out to ensure the hydrants remain operational. The fire authority should be consulted.

SUMMARY

123 In recent years few people have been injured by fires in paper mills, but every year there are a number of fires requiring the attendance of the fire service and causing considerable financial loss. There are also hundreds more which are adequately dealt with by paper mill first-aid fire-fighters. It must not be forgotten that the potential for multiple fatalities in a major fire remains.

124 To help reduce this toll it is vital that senior managers are committed to preventing fires and explosions and ensuring that workpeople are not put at risk, should either occur. The risks require assessment and managing to ensure effective control. Written emergency arrangements are an essential part of such control. Key staff should be fully involved and safety representatives consulted.

125 The aim is to stop a fire starting and, if one does occur, to enable people to escape safely and to prevent it spreading. Day-to-day control is essential to keep the quantity of flammables to a minimum, to ensure safe handling of flammable materials, to exclude sources of ignition and to keep up standards of housekeeping. Means of escape need to be identified and kept free of obstruction; exits need to be immediately available for use in emergency.

126 All staff need to be adequately trained so that they are able to play their part in minimising fire risks and know what to do if fire breaks out or other emergencies occur.

127 Everyone needs to be vigilant in their own interest and that of other people.

APPENDIX 1: SUMMARIES OF FIRE-RELATED INCIDENTS IN THE PAPER INDUSTRY

1 Contractors were using oxy-acetylene cutting equipment on a papermaking machine which was being modified. They had been using foam polystyrene slabs as kneeling pads. These had been ignited by sparks and half an hour after the contractors had left for a tea break a fire was discovered at the base of the paper machine. As the felt was dry and as the drying hood and roof linings were also flammable the fire spread rapidly. There were no injuries but there was considerable damage to the building, paper machine and computer control equipment.

2 About 2500 tonnes of waste paper in bales were stacked in an open yard, to a height of about 5 m. The fire was discovered in one corner, and was attacked unsuccessfully by employees with water extinguishers.

The case was recorded as spontaneous combustion. Paper itself will not ignite spontaneously unless its temperature rises to 200°C or more in a substantial quantity of material, ie many tens of kilos. Waste paper bales contain impurities, sometimes quite a lot of them, and it is possible that a quantity of reactive material was trapped inside a bale, for example paint or linseed oil soaked rags. In such a situation, the high wind on the day of the fire could have been enough to convert a slow smouldering in the inside of a bale into flaming combustion.

3 More than 10 000 tonnes of newsprint were destroyed in a warehouse fire. The reels were stacked on end to a height of around 6 m. Paper reels in good condition present a hard surface that is difficult to ignite. However, reels often sustain minor damage making fire easier to start. Once a fire has started, the 'chimneys' between reels enhance the speed and spread of it. Air enters at the bottom at high speed due to the small gap and the chimney effect of the spaces between reels gives very rapid burning. It is estimated that peak heat outputs in this fire were in excess of 1000MW. It is estimated that a 7 m high stack would burn roughly four times as fast as a 5 m stack.

In this case the roof was breached at an early stage allowing heat and smoke to vent upwards. If this had not occurred, the hot gases would have travelled sideways under the roof giving a rapid sideways spread of fire which would have been difficult to control.

4 A tissue mill warehouse sustained severe damage when a propane-fuelled fork lift truck caught fire. Pieces of paper were caught beneath the truck and sparks and heat from the truck's exhaust system ignited the trapped paper. The fire burnt through the hydraulic oil hoses and the propane feed pipe, with subsequent ignition of escaping oil and gas intensifying the flame. The fire spread to the nearby large reels of tissue paper.

Earlier the same day another propane-fuelled fork lift truck had caught fire. The fire had started in the engine compartment of the truck when arcing due to a short circuit ignited the electrical insulation covering the wiring. This fire was successfully put out using dry powder and CO_2 extinguishers.

5   A contractor was burning and cutting off redundant steelwork adjacent to a papermaking machine. There was inadequate segregation from the machine or control of sparks. Paper in the calender pit was ignited and the fire spread to the roof of the building.

6   There was a solvent explosion and fire in a coating laminator. The initial explosion was followed by a sequence of explosions in the evaporating ovens and extraction ducting with a small fire at the coating head. The ignition source was unknown but solvent levels were above the Lower Explosive Limit. There was no monitoring of the air flow.

7   Two paper machine crewmen were detained in hospital for 36 hours as a result of inhaling smoke and other products of combustion while using hoses to fight fire in the drier hood of a paper-making machine. The cause of the outbreak of the fire was not established but the copious quantity of smoke appeared to result from rapid burning of the synthetic textile drier felt. One of the men affected had previous fire-fighting experience; the other had no previous experience or training in fire-fighting.

8   Two operatives engaged in first-aid fire-fighting on a paper-making machine suffered breathing difficulties after another operative attempting to fight the fire released the contents of a dry powder extinguisher into their faces. This latter operative had not apparently been trained in the use of such extinguishers.

9   There was a fire and explosion in a de-inking switchroom. This was caused by a contractor's electrician attempting to replace fuses into a live switch cabinet on completion of testing work. The interlock on the isolator handle was faulty.

10   The following example from the USA is included as it illustrates the extreme consequences which can arise from a paper mill fire.

Employees were using an abrasive wheel grinder to cut a small hole in the steel roof of a bale storage building. Welding, using an arc and oxygen acetylene torch, was also used in the work. A fire started in the 9 m high by 7 m thick by 1.2 m long compressed waste tissue paper bales weighing 225 to 320 kg which were located in the building. The bales were stacked five high. The company's fire department was called and the 36 heads of the sprinkler system were activated. The community fire company also responded.

A fire-fighter and the fire captain advanced into the fire area with a charged hose line. The water sprayed on to the stacked bales rendered them unstable and caused them to topple, trapping the two employees. Seven others entered the building in a rescue attempt. Three of these were also trapped by additional falling bales. Forklifts were used to remove the bales, and lumber pieces were used to shore up other bales. Three fire fighters, including the captain, died as well as two other employees.

APPENDIX 2: LEGAL REQUIREMENTS

1   European Community Directives to encourage improvements in the safety and health of workers at work are being implemented by means of the Management of Health and Safety at Work Regulations 1992 and the Workplace (Health, Safety and Welfare) Regulations 1992. At the time of writing, the Home Office and the Scottish Office aim to make fire safety legislation - the Fire Precautions (Places of Work) Regulations in 1995 with the legislation coming into effect in 1996.

2   The Health and Safety at Work etc Act 1974 (Reference 35) and relevant Regulations cover the provision of 'process fire precautions' which are intended to prevent the outbreak of fire or mitigate the consequences if one occurs. Matters falling within the scope of the Act include the storage of flammable materials, the control of flammable vapours, standards of housekeeping, safe systems of work, the control of courses of ignition and provision of appropriate training. In paper mills the Act will be enforced by HSE inspectors (see under Health and Safety Executive in the telephone directory).

3   The Fire Precautions Act 1971 (Reference 34) is the responsibility of the Home Office and the Scottish Office (The Home Departments) and is normally enforced by fire authorities. For Crown premises, enforcement is undertaken by the Crown Premises Inspection Group of HM Fire Service Inspectorates of the Home Departments. It deals with 'general fire precautions' and includes the provision of means of escape, means for fighting fire, means of giving warning in case of fire, and the training of staff in fire safety. The location of your fire authority can be found in the telephone directory.

4   In England and Wales the licensing authority for the keeping of petroleum spirit or petroleum mixtures is normally the county council or in metropolitan counties and London, the Fire and Civil Defence Authority; in Scotland it is normally the local regional or islands council.

The Health and Safety
at Work etc Act 1974

5   The Health and Safety at Work etc Act 1974 (HSW Act) is concerned with securing the health, safety and welfare of persons at work, and with protecting people who are not at work, from risks to their health and safety arising from work activities. For further details see References 35 and 37. In terms of fire precautions the HSW Act and relevant Regulations, eg the Highly Flammable Liquids and Liquefied Petroleum Gases Regulations 1972 and the Electricity at Work Regulations 1989, are used to control the keeping and use of flammable substances and to control sources of ignition.

6   Section 6 of the HSW Act applies to manufacturers, importers and suppliers of substances who have to ensure, so far as is reasonably practicable, that the substances are safe and without risks to health. They need among other things to identify the potential hazards and to provide information about these hazards and the conditions necessary for safe use, eg precautions in handling and storage. In the case of flammable substances, this information

. . . .

Page 35 Paper and Board Industry Advisory Committee

should include a description of the inherent hazards of fire and the expected consequences if the substance is exposed to fire or excessive heat. The section places similar obligations on designers, manufacturers, importers and suppliers of articles for use at work and on those who erect and install them. Further guidance is available in References 5 and 37.

7 Inspectors enforcing the HSW Act have the power of entry into premises without prior notice and can issue notices requiring specified improvements or prohibiting the use of substances, plant, equipment or buildings.

8 The enforcing authority should be notified immediately, for example by telephone, if someone is killed or suffers a major injury as a result of an accident arising out of or in connection with work. Immediate notification is also needed if an explosion or fire results in the stoppage of plant or suspension of normal work for more than 24 hours where the explosion or fire was due to the ignition of process materials, their by-products (including waste) or finished products. This has to be followed up by a written report on Form F 2508. A written report should also be sent following an accident at work if the injury causes incapacity for more than three days. For details of the Reporting of Injuries, Diseases and Dangerous Occurrences Regulations 1985, see Reference 38.

The Fire Precautions Act 1971

9 The Fire Precautions Act 1971 as amended by the Fire Safety and Safety of Places of Sport Act 1987 is the principal instrument for fire safety in factories and associated offices, and is designed to ensure the adequate provision of means of escape in case of fire and related fire precautions.

10 Inspectors, usually uniformed members of the local authority fire brigade enforcing the Fire Precautions Act have the power of entry into premises without notice at any reasonable time and can issue notices requiring specified improvements. They may also serve a notice prohibiting or restricting the use of any premises, (whether or not it requires a fire certificate) if the conditions are or will become, in the case of fire, such that they present a serious risk to people on the premises.

Premises requiring a fire certificate

11 A fire certificate is generally required if more than 20 people are at work in the premises at any one time or if more than ten people are at work at any one time elsewhere than on the ground floor.

12 A fire certificate will also be required in a factory if explosive or highly flammable materials are stored or used either in or under the premises.

13 Application for a fire certificate should be made by the owner/occupier of the premises on Form FP1 (Rev) which can be obtained from the local authority fire brigade. It is an offence not to apply for a fire certificate if one is required.

14 While awaiting the outcome of the application for a fire certificate the occupier of the premises has a statutory duty to ensure that:

(a) the means of escape in case of fire can be safely and effectively used at all times when there are people in the premises;

(b) the fire-fighting equipment is maintained in efficient working order; and

(c) all staff are trained in what to do in the event of fire.

15 The fire certificate will be tailored specifically to the premises in question. It may impose requirements for maintenance of the means of escape and associated fire precautions, the training of staff, limiting the number of people who may be in the premises at any one time and other precautions that have to be observed.

16 Normally the occupier of the premises is responsible for ensuring adherence to all the requirements of a fire certificate.

17 The law requires that the fire certificate is kept on the premises to which it relates. It should be available for reference or inspection at all times.

18 The fire authority should be informed in advance if it is proposed to:

(a) make a material extension of, or material structural alteration to, the premises; or

(b) make a material alteration in the internal arrangement of the premises or in the furniture or equipment with which the premises are provided; or

(c) begin to store or use or materially increase the storage or use of, explosive or highly flammable materials.

19 Firms that do not employ sufficient people to require a fire certificate and do not use or store explosive or highly flammable materials are subject to Section 9A of the Fire Precautions Act 1971 which states that: *all premises to which it applies shall be provided with such means of escape in case of fire and such means for fighting fire as may reasonably be required in the circumstances of the case.* Normally the occupier of the premises is responsible for ensuring that this statutory duty is complied with.

Multi-occupied premises

20 In the case of multi-occupied premises the owner will be responsible for the application for a fire certificate and for the provision and maintenance of general fire safety measures. Occupiers will, however, normally be responsible for specific fire safety measures, eg keeping exit doors and exit routes available and free from obstruction in the relevant premises, and in those common or shared parts of the building over which they have control.

Further guidance

21 Attention is drawn to the publications issued by the Home Office and The Scottish Office Home and Health Department (References 1, 29 and 36).

Fire Services Act 1947

22 This Act requires every fire authority to make provision for fire-fighting purposes by training, equipping and ensuring that there are efficient arrangements for dealing with calls for assistance and for summoning members of the fire brigade. Efficient arrangements for obtaining information about the character of buildings and other property for fire-fighting purposes within the area must be made. Management will be able to offer useful advice about the site and/or the processes carried out. It is therefore essential that close liaison is established and maintained between the management of the mill and the local authority fire brigade so that in the event of an emergency the fire brigade is familiar with the site and all its hazards. Managements should also note that under Section 30 of the Act the senior fire brigade officer present at the scene is in overall charge of the incident.

Petroleum (Consolidation) Act 1928 and the Petroleum (Mixtures) Order 1929

23 With certain minor exceptions the Act prohibits the keeping of petroleum spirit unless a petroleum spirit licence is in force.

24 Petroleum spirit kept under licence needs to be kept in accordance with the conditions of the licence. A notice setting out any conditions to be observed by employees should be kept prominently posted.

25 Any petroleum spirit kept in any place should have attached to it or displayed near the vessel containing it a label shown in conspicuous characters the words 'PETROLEUM SPIRIT - HIGHLY FLAMMABLE'.

26 The Petroleum (Mixtures) Order 1929 applies all of the provisions of the Act, including licensing, to a large range of mixtures whether liquid, viscous or solid. The required label is 'PETROLEUM MIXTURES GIVING OFF A FLAMMABLE HEAVY VAPOUR'.

Building regulations

27 In England and Wales the Building Regulations 1991 apply to new buildings and to building work such as the erection, extension or material alteration of an existing building. They also apply where there is a material change of use.

28 The Regulations impose fire safety requirements covering such matters as:

(a) means of escape in case of fire;

(b) structural stability;

(c) fire resistance of elements of structure;

(d) compartmentalisation to inhibit fire-spread;

(e) reduction of spread of flame over surfaces of walls and ceilings;

(f) space separation between buildings to reduce the risk of fire spread from one building to another; and

(g) access for fire appliances and assistance to the fire brigade.

29 The standard of provision is related to the size and height of the building and the use to which it is put. The Regulations also impose requirements as to means of escape in case of fire.

30 Where it is proposed to erect a new building, to carry out building work as described in paragraph 28 or to make a material change of use, application should be made to the building control department of the relevant local authority.

31 In Scotland the Building Standards (Scotland) Regulations 1990 apply. These contain detailed requirements relating to means of escape in case of fire, structural fire precautions and assistance to the fire brigade and, like the Regulations in England and Wales, are related to the size and height of the building and the use to which it is put. The Regulations also contain different requirements for the storage of materials that give rise to different fire hazards.

Other regulations **32** The Dangerous Substances (Notification and Marking of Sites) Regulations 1990 require those in charge of a site containing 25 tonnes or more of dangerous substances (as defined in the Chemicals (Hazard Information and Packaging for Supply) Regulations 1994 to notify the local fire/enforcing authority and also to erect specified warning signs (Figure 3a) at such access points as will give adequate warning to fire fighters that dangerous substances are present on a site. Also, from 1 March 1993 site operators will need to erect appropriate warning signs (Figure 3b) at locations within the site, where directed to do so by an inspector. For further information see Reference 39.

Figure 3a
Access warning sign

Figure 3b
Examples of location warning signs

33 The Notification of Installations Handling Hazardous Substances Regulations 1982 apply to premises with specified quantities of particular substances, such as 25 tonnes of liquid petroleum gas, and require such sites to be notified to HSE.

34 The Chemicals (Hazard Information and Packaging for Supply) Regulations 1994 (CHIP 2) provide for the classification, packaging and labelling of dangerous substances and are designed to protect people and the environment from the ill-effects of chemicals. They apply, with some exceptions, to substances (as defined in the HSW Act) supplied or consigned for conveyance by road in a package, and which are dangerous for supply or for conveyance. See Reference 40 for further details.

35 The Highly Flammable Liquids and Liquefied Petroleum Gases Regulations 1972 apply to flammable liquids which have a flash point of less than 32°Celsius (90° Fahrenheit). They provide for safe storage, transfer and use including the avoidance of sources of ignition where concentrations of flammable vapour may be present. Specific control measures for liquid petroleum gas storage and use are also covered.

APPENDIX 3: SELECTING THE APPROPRIATE EXTINGUISHER

1   There are four main classes of fire classes - A, B, C and D. Only classes A-C will be relevant for the paper industry.

Class 'A' fires   2   Fires involving solid materials, usually of an organic nature, eg wood or paper in which combustion normally takes place with the formation of glowing embers. Class A fires occur frequently and it will be appropriate to provide fire fighting equipment suitable for this class of fire. Water, foam (other than protein foam) and multi-purpose powder are the most effective media for extinguishing these fires. Water and foam are usually considered the most suitable media, and the appropriate equipment would be hose reels or water-type extinguishers or extinguishers containing fluoroprotein foam (FP), aqueous film protein foam (AFFF) or film forming fluoroprotein foam (FFFP)

3   If hose reels are installed they should be located where they are conspicuous and always accessible. Their distribution should be such that with not more than 45 m of hose, no part of the area to be protected is more than 6m from the nozzle of the reel when the hose is fully run out. Hose reel installations should conform with the appropriate recommendations in British Standards 5306: Part I (Reference 41) and 5274 (Reference 42).

4   If portable fire extinguishers are installed, they should be provided and allocated to accord with the recommendations contained in British Standard 5306: Part 3: Clause 5.2 which deals with extinguishers suitable for Class A fires (Reference 41).

Class 'B' fires   5   Fires involving flammable liquids or liquefiable solids (greases and fats). In buildings or parts of buildings where there is a risk of fire involving flammable liquid it will usually be appropriate to provide portable fire extinguishers of foam, carbon dioxide (CO_2), or powder types. Care should be taken when using gaseous extinguishers, as the fumes and products of combustion may be hazardous in confined spaces. For environmental reasons it is recommended that the provision of halon extinguishers should be avoided where other suitable extinguishing media are available. Table 1 of Clause 5.3 of British Standard 5306: Part 3 (Reference 41) gives guidance on the minimum scale of provision of various extinguishing media for dealing with a fire involving exposed surfaces of contained liquid.

Class 'C' fires   6   Fires involving gases: No special extinguishers are made for dealing with fires involving gases. While dry powder extinguishers are capable of putting out small fires, normally the only effective action against such fires is to stop the flow of gas. There would be a risk of an explosion if a fire involving escaping gas were to be extinguished before the supply could be cut off.

Fires involving live electrical equipment   7   Extinguishers provided specifically for the protection of electrical risks should be of the dry powder or CO_2 type. While some extinguishers containing aqueous solutions such as AFFF may meet the requirements of the electrical conductivity test of BS5423 (Reference 43) they may not sufficiently reduce the danger of conductivity along wetted surfaces such as the floor. Consequently such extinguishers should not be provided specifically for the protection of electrical risks and should not be provided in close proximity to live electrical equipment.

General   **8**   Fire extinguishers should conform to British Standard 5423 (Reference 43). Those which do are approved by the British Standards Institution and certified under the British Approvals for Fire Equipment (BAFE) scheme. Conforming equipment bears the Loss Prevention Council (LPC) or BAFE marks of approval. All extinguishers should be installed and maintained as outlined in BS5306: Part 3 (Reference 41). It is recommended that the contract maintenance of portable fire extinguishers is entrusted to a competent person, such as a BAFE-registered firm.

9   In some circumstances it may be more appropriate to use a fire blanket rather than an extinguisher, eg to deal with a cooker fire in the early stages, or to smother a fire involving a person's clothing. Such blankets should be to BS6575 (Reference 44) and be asbestos free.

10   Staff who receive training in use of hand fire-fighting equipment should be instructed on the different types of fire described above and the appropriate type of equipment.

Figure 4 Fire extinguishers

WATER

RED

EXTINGUISHING ACTION
Mainly by cooling the burning material.

Class of fire
Class A

DANGER: Do not use on live electrical equipment, burning fats or oils.

Method of use
The jet should be directed at the base of the flames and kept moving across the area of the fire. Any hot spots should be sought out after the main fire is out.

FOAM (Protein P) Type

CREAM

EXTINGUISHING ACTION
Forms a blanket of foam over the surface of the burning liquid and smothers the fire.

Class of fire
Class B

DANGER: Do not use on live electrical equipment.

Method of use
The jet should not be aimed directly onto the liquid. Where the liquid on fire is in a container the jet should be directed at the edge of the container or on a nearby surface above the burning liquid. The foam should be allowed to build up so that it flows across the liquid.

AQUEOUS FILM FORMING FOAM (AFFF)

CREAM

Film-forming Fluoroprotein
foam (FFFP)

Fluoroprotein foam (FP)

EXTINGUISHING ACTION
Forms a fire extinguishing water film on the surface of the burning liquid. Has a cooling action with a wider extinguishing application than water on solid combustable materials.

Class of fire
Classes A and B

DANGER: Some extinguishers of this type are not suitable for use on live electrical equipment.

Method of use
For Class A fires the directions for water extinguishers should be followed.

For Class B fires the directions for foam extinguishers should be followed.

POWDER

BLUE

EXTINGUISHING ACTION
Knocks down flames.

Class of fire
Class B

Safe on live electrical equipment although does not readily penetrate spaces inside equipment. A fire may re-ignite.

Method of use
The discharge nozzle should be directed at the base of the flames and with a rapid sweeping motion the flames should be driven towards the far edge until the flames are out. If the extinguisher has a shut-off control the air should then be allowed to clear; if the flames reappear the procedure should be repeated.

WARNING: Powder has a limited cooling effect and care should be taken to ensure the fire does not re-ignite.

POWDER (Multi-purpose)

BLUE

EXTINGUISHING ACTION
Knocks down flames and on burning solids melts down to form a skin smothering the fire. Has some cooling effect.

Class of fire
Classes A and B

Safe on live electrical equipment although does not readily penetrate spaces inside equipment. A fire may re-ignite.

Method of use
The discharge nozzle should be directed at the base of the flames and with a rapid sweeping motion the flames should be driven towards the far edge until the flames are out. If the extinguisher has a shut-off control the air should then be allowed to clear; if the flames reappear the procedure should be repeated.

WARNING: Powder has a limited cooling effect and care should be taken to ensure the fire does not re-ignite.

CARBON DIOXIDE (CO₂)

BLACK

EXTINGUISHING ACTION

Vapourising liquid gas which smothers flames by displacement of oxygen in the air.

Class of fire

Class B

Safe and clean to use on live electrical equipment.

Method of use

The discharge horn should be directed at the base of the flames and the jet kept moving across the area of the fire.

WARNING: CO₂ has a limited cooling effect and care should be taken to ensure the fire does not re-ignite.

DANGER: Fumes from CO₂ extinguishers can be harmful to users in confined spaces. The area should therefore be ventilated as soon as the fire has been extinguished.

HOSE REEL

RED

EXTINGUISHING ACTION

Mainly by cooling the burning material.

Class of fire

Class A

DANGER: Do not use on live electrical equipment.

Method of use

The jet should be aimed at the base of the flames and kept moving across the area of the fire. If an isolating valve is fitted it should be opened before the hose is unreeled.

FIRE BLANKET

RED

EXTINGUISHING ACTION

Smothering

Class of fire

Classes A and B

Light duty - Suitable for burning clothing and small fires involving burning liquids.
Heavy duty - Suitable for industrial use. Resistant to penetration by molten materials.

Method of use

The blanket should be placed carefully over the fire and the hands shielded from the fire. Care should be taken that the flames are not wafted towards the user or bystanders.

British Standard 5423 recommends that extinguishers should be (a) predominantly red with a colour coded area; (b) predominantly coloured coded; or (c) of self-coloured metal with a colour coded area.

APPENDIX 4: PERMIT TO WORK

1 In operating a permit-to-work system the following principles should be observed:

(a) The information given in the permit should be clear and unambiguous;

(b) It should specify precisely and in detail the item of plant on which work is to be carried out, the nature of the operations, the point at which welding or hot work is to take place and the precautions which should be taken to ensure safety of personnel;

(c) The permit should specify the time at which it comes into operation, the time by which it expires and any particular conditions under which all work should cease even though the time limit for the certificate has not expired;

(d) The person issuing the permit should be satisfied by personal inspection, that all the action specified as necessary has in fact been taken;

(e) The person issuing the certificate should have the technical knowledge not only to appreciate the existence of hazards and the precautions to be taken, but also the authority to require responsible people to make safety recommendations on matters of which they have special knowledge and to co-ordinate the duties of all concerned;

(f) Permits should be monitored by management to ensure that they are being correctly issued and the conditions are being complied with.

2 The permit-to-work procedure outlined above is for general guidance and should be adopted to suit particular needs. A possible layout is given below.

PLANT DETAILS (Location, identifying number etc) **WORK TO BE DONE**	**ACCEPTANCE OF CERTIFICATE**	I have read and understood this certificate and will undertake to work in accordance with the conditions in it. Signed Date Time
EQUIPMENT TO BE USED (eg electric arc welding set, abrasive cut-off disc)	**COMPLETION OF WORK**	The work has been completed and all persons under my supervision, materials and equipment withdrawn. Signed Date Time
CLEANING LOCATION The area has been cleared of flammable and combustible materials which could be ignited by the activity, falling slag or sparks, and/or suitable coverings have been provided (specify which). **FIRE-FIGHTING** Suitable fire extinguishers/hoses have been placed adjacent to the work (specify which). Persons doing work have been adequately trained in their use/trained fire watcher present.*	**REQUEST FOR EXTENSION**	I have re-examined the plant details above and confirm that the certificate may be extended to expire at: Further precautions: Signed Date Time
	INSPECTION OF LOCATION IMMEDIATELY AFTER WORK	I have examined the work location and there is no sign of ignition/smouldering of any substance. Signed Date Time
CONDITIONS Work should cease in the event of the following:	**INSPECTION OF LOCATION ONE HOUR AFTER WORK**	I have examined the work location and there is no sign of ignition/smouldering of any substance. Signed Date Time

I CERTIFY THAT I HAVE PERSONALLY EXAMINED THE PLANT DETAILED ABOVE AND SATISFIED MYSELF THAT THE ABOVE PARTICULARS ARE CORRECT.
 	
Signed
   Date   Time
	THE PERMIT TO WORK IS NOW CANCELLED. A NEW PERMIT WILL BE REQUIRED IF WORK IS TO CONTINUE.
	
	Signed
	   Date Time	

* Delete option not applicable

APPENDIX 5: FIRE-RESISTING STRUCTURES

Functions of fire-resisting construction

1   The provision of fire-resisting construction to appropriate standards, and properly located, can contribute greatly to the safety of life and property in the event of fire. There is the added advantage that successful containment of any fire will minimise any subsequent loss of production.

2   Among the specific uses of fire-resisting construction are:

(a) the protection of escape routes from the effects of fire to enable people to leave the building safely;

(b) the division of the building into compartments in order to contain any fire which may occur;

(c) the separation of areas of high fire-risk from the remainder of the building; and

(d) the protection from fire of load bearing and structural members to minimise the risk of early collapse of the building.

Test standards

3   Fire-resisting or fire resistance means the ability of a component of construction of a building to satisfy for a stated period of time (eg 30 minutes) some or all of the appropriate criteria (ie integrity, insulation and stability/load bearing capacity) specified in the relevant part of British Standards.

4   In existing premises, it may not be possible to ascertain the fire resistance of some elements of structure and a judgement will need to be made on whether the fire resistance is acceptable in the particular circumstances.

Circumstances under which fire-resisting construction may be required

5   Fire-resisting construction will generally be required by the Building Control Authority in new or materially altered premises to satisfy Parts B1 and B3 of the Building Regulations (means of escape in case of fire and internal fire spread, structures).

6   Fire-resisting construction may be required by the fire authority to protect the means of escape in existing buildings (but not in excess of that required by Building Regulations unless the means of escape are not satisfactory by virtue of matters not required to be shown for the purposes of Building Regulation approval).

7   Fire-resisting construction may be required by HSE in order to separate high fire-risk storage areas from the remainder of the building.

8   Fire-resisting construction may be required by the insurers to provide fire-resisting compartmentalisation to limit the spread of fire and consequent property losses.

APPENDIX 6: EMERGENCY PROCEDURES

1   When fire breaks out or the fire alarm sounds personnel need to be clear about the procedures to be followed. Fire fighters are at increased risk if they have to enter a smoke-logged building with machinery still in motion. However in some circumstances there can be increased risk from personnel stopping to shut down large machinery.

2   The principle is that mill personnel should not be put at risk. Where a fire is immediately threatening, the mill must be evacuated as rapidly as possible. Only if it can be done safely should personnel stay to shut down the paper machine. The decision on what action to take should be made by a designated person who has the knowledge and authority to make an appropriate decision.

3   Mills will have to draw up their own procedures, taking into account the physical environment of the paper machine, the type of fire alarm provided and the level of supervision which is available. An example of the emergency procedure drawn up by one mill is given on page 49. This example is intended to be illustrative and should not be considered as a model procedure. Individual arrangements are likely to vary from mill to mill.

FIRE ACTION - PAPER MACHINES

Emergency evacuation procedures for crews

Continuous alarm

The sounding of a continuous alarm is intended to warn you that a fire has started in your department. In the event of a continuous alarm sounding, the following action should be taken:

Either:

1 Shut the paper machine in a controlled manner prior to evacuation if safe to do so:
   - closing down all extraction fans
   - flushing stock and starch lines
   - parting rolls
   - setting down steam pressures to minimum

Or:

2 Crash shut the paper machine in the event of extensive fire in danger of rapid spread but only if safe to do so.

Or:

3 In the event of a fire in the dryer section take the following action prior to evacuation if safe to do so:
   - set cylinders to crawl on all sections of the machine
   - reduce steam pressures to minimum

OR, IF IT IS NOT SAFE TO DO ANY OF THE ABOVE:

4 Evacuate with the machine left running and report this fact as a priority at the assembly point.

Intermittent alarm

The sounding of an intermittent alarm is intended to warn you that a fire has started in another department. In the event of an intermittent alarm you should prepare to evacuate if necessary under the instruction of your shift supervisor.

Duties of the machine shift supervisor

In the event of the alarm sounding, the machine shift supervisor should:

   - control evacuation of the area and ensure the safety of the crews
   - advise personnel in the boiler house.

APPENDIX 7: COATING AND LAMINATING PROCEDURES

1   These processes almost always use flammable solvents and they therefore pose serious fire/explosion risks. The strict requirements of the Highly Flammable Liquids and Liquefied Petroleum Gases Regulations 1972 will apply. Sources of ignition should be avoided and smoking strictly prohibited. Wherever possible substitution with less flammable materials should be considered, taking into account any health hazards.

2   Machines on which flammable solvents are used should be separated from storage areas and other parts of the building by partitioning with a fire resistance of not less than half an hour.

3   Where mixing has to be done in-house this should normally be carried out in a special-purpose fire resisting room (separate from the storage area) provided with mechanical ventilation.

4   Where vapour may enter the atmosphere, local exhaust ventilation should be provided to remove the vapour from as close to the source as possible, in order to reduce the risk of fire and explosion and to reduce employee exposure to solvent vapours. The workroom itself should have a good standard of general ventilation.

5   In order to reduce the amount of solvent vapour entering the room and minimise possible spillage, supply containers etc should be kept covered. It is preferable to pump solvent to machines and to return any excess solvent to storage via an enclosed system. Where it is necessary to break and remake a connection frequently, for example when making a colour change, a sealed end coupling is preferred. Where possible, pipe runs should be in the open air and suitable shut-off valves should be provided. A manual emergency shut-off valve is recommended where a pipe enters a process building. Pipework and fittings should be to a suitable standard, for example ANSI B31.3, and arrangements should be made for routine maintenance including leak testing of pipework, fittings, storage tanks etc.

6   Highly flammable liquids should not be kept or moved in open-topped vessels. Only properly constructed vessels should be used for mixing and dispensing. Empty or partly used drums of solvent are still hazardous and should not be allowed to accumulate around the machine. Highly flammable liquids such as toluene should not be used for floor cleaning.

7   The amount of vapour produced by coatings increases rapidly with temperature so they should be used at as low a temperature as possible. The normal working temperature for a coating should not be exceeded.

8   Any electrical equipment on the press or in the surrounding area should be constructed to a suitable explosion protection standard to avoid any risk of ignition (Reference 21). Powered lift trucks should not be used close to machines unless suitably protected (Reference 22). Where a local exhaust ventilation system is provided for the removal of solvent vapour, the fan motor should not be located in the path of the vapour and the duct work should be fire-resisting.

9   The generation of static electricity is a problem, especially at those laminators/varnishers which handle plastic or other insulating materials, including many papers. In particular, charging of unearthed metal parts as the web passes over cylinders and rollers etc can lead to spark discharges liable to ignite volatile solvents, and people may become charged by induction and by transfer of charge from the web. They may also become charged by walking on an insulating floor or by removing an outer garment. Operations such as pouring, mixing and pumping organic solvents can also generate static electricity. The following precautions should be taken (see also BS5958: Part 2 - Reference 46).

(a)   The generation of static electricity from solvents and other low conductivity liquids should be minimised by avoiding free fall of liquids and restricting pumping speed. For liquids with conductivity up to and including 50 plcosiemen per metre (pS/m) the flow velocity in a pipe should not exceed 1 metre per second if a second phase, commonly water, is present. Water may be present even if not deliberately introduced eg condensate and so a flow velocity above 1 metre per second should only be considered if there is no possibility of this; only in these circumstances should velocities up to 7 metres per second by considered. Consideration should also be given to the use of anti-static additives to increase conductivity; these reduce the likelihood that a solvent will accumulate a static charge but they will not control static electricity from other sources such as those mentioned above;

(b)   Vessels, containers, pipework, hoses and plant etc which may become electro-statically charged, either directly or by induction, should be conductive and bonded together and/or earthed. On fixed plant, the resistance to earth of all metal or conducting parts should be checked at the commissioning stage and regularly thereafter;

(c)   All personnel who may come into contact with a potentially flammable atmosphere should wear anti-static footwear; the resistance of footwear while being worn may be measured by means of a personnel resistance monitor. Preferably only outer clothing made from natural fibres should be worn, as synthetic fibres can generate static. Although there is no evidence that wearing synthetic underwear can cause a static problem, natural fibres are recommended because injury in the event of fire or explosion is likely to be less severe. Outer clothing such as pullovers and overalls should not be removed in areas where flammable vapours may be present. It should be remembered that even at a level where electrostatic charges cannot be felt, they are capable of igniting some solvent vapours.

(d) Floors in hazardous areas (Reference 21) should not be highly insulating; for example concrete would be suitable. They should be kept free of insulating deposits;

(e) Electrostatic eliminators, of a design incapable of producing incendive sparks, should be used on any insulating web-fed material; passive, high voltage and radioactive types are available. This equipment should, where relevant, be constructed to a suitable explosion protection standard to avoid a risk of ignition, and it should be kept clean and properly maintained;

(f) Devices for applying a high electrostatic charge are sometimes used, normally in conjunction with a static eliminator to neutralise the charge before the web moves forward. These devices should be incapable of producing sparks, be constructed to a suitable explosion protection standard, and be kept clean and properly maintained;

(g) In order to avoid the possibility of incendive sparks, the use of highly insulating plastic materials should be avoided in hazardous areas. In particular, powders should not be discharged from plastic bags or liners in the vicinity of flammable atmospheres;

(h) The manual addition of powders or low conductivity liquids to vessels containing a potentially flammable atmosphere should be avoided.

10 Fixed fire detection and extinguishing systems such as carbon dioxide systems designed for both manual and automatic operation are recommended (see paragraphs 115 and 116). When such equipment is operating, further flammable solvents should be prevented from entering dryers/extract ducting, and dampers should normally be fully shut to prevent the extinguishing medium being removed.

11 Particular care should be taken to ensure that dryers incorporate all necessary safeguards to minimise the risk of solvent/air or gas/air explosions, and to mitigate the consequences of an explosion, should one occur. For example:

(a) Solvent concentrations in dryers and associated duct work should not exceed 25% of the lower flammable limit (LFL) under all operating conditions (but see sub-paragraph (e) below). This can normally be achieved by an air flow of 60 m^3 at 16°C for every litre of solvent evaporated. The concentration should be checked by calculation and measurement during commissioning or if the operating conditions are altered. Also, instruments can be used to monitor the solvent concentration in the dryer continuously. The exhaust or inlet ventilation rate, and where appropriate recirculation rate, should be monitored by a differential pressure device or airflow switch. Detection of inadequate exhaust should automatically stop the process and safely shut down the means of heating. In addition a clear, audible warning should sound automatically. Visible warning may also be provided;

(b) Operation of an emergency stop button should safely shut down the means of heating, but the exhaust ventilation should continue to operate;

(c) The movement of the coated web (not a dry web) should be possible only if adequate exhaust ventilation has been proved;

(d) Adequate explosion relief should be provided on dryers and on associated large-scale duct work;

(e) Exceptionally, some dryers have been designed to operate above 25% of the LFL where there is continuous monitoring. Operation above 25% of the LFL should not be attempted unless the nature of the process ensures that vapour concentrations within the dryer change slowly relative to the effective detection and activation times of the continuous monitor and safety shut-down interlock systems. Under no circumstances should a dryer be operated above a solvent concentration of 50% of the LFL. Such fixed vapour detection equipment should:

(i)   be suitable for the solvents to be measured;

(ii) be calibrated for the solvents concerned, regularly tested and recalibrated, and well maintained;

(iii) normally sample at points within the dryer and/or duct work where the vapour concentration is likely to be highest;

(iv) operate an audible and visible alarm if the solvent vapour concentration at separate sampling points exceeds the normal operating limit;

(v)   have two independent reliable instruments measuring the solvent concentration at separate sampling points, each of which can safely shut down the process and the dryer's means of heating before the solvent vapour concentration rises above a pre-determined maximum (which should not be above 50% of the LFL);

(vi) be arranged to open any modulated dampers fully in the event of a malfunction in the continuous monitoring system;

(vii) automatically and continuously monitor and record the progression of solvent vapour concentration with time;

(f) Where there is a solvent recovery unit a damper should be provided in the dryer extract duct to isolate the unit from any fire on the machine or in the ducting. *Fire safety in the printing industry* gives guidance on the safety of these units (Reference 48).

12 Vapour detection equipment is sometimes provided near machines in order to detect escapes of solvent into the general atmosphere of the workroom. Where such equipment is not provided, regular routine measurements should be considered to ensure that the atmosphere is maintained below 25% of the LFL. One method of doing this would be to use a portable flammable gas detector to check for escapes of vapour at flanges, valves, pump seals and other potential sources of leaks.

13 Where appropriate, automatic viscosity measuring equipment should be provided on the machine or it should be possible to take samples from a position at the side of the machine rather than from between the units.

14 Where highly flammable liquids are used to clean rollers, cylinders and ancillary equipment, the operation should preferably be done in a proprietary solvent-cleaning machine fitted with exhaust ventilation. In other cases cleaning should take place in a purpose-designed booth; the enclosure and extract ducting should be fire-resisting and the electric motor driving the extraction fan should not be in the path of the vapour. Where rollers/cylinders are cleaned by hand on the machine, only small volumes should be applied in well-ventilated conditions. The solvents should be kept in non-spill containers.

REFERENCES

1 *Guide to fire precautions in existing places of work that require a fire certificate Factories, offices, shops and railway premises* Fire Precautions Act 1971. Home Office and The Scottish Office Home and Health Department. HMSO 1993 ISBN 0 11 341079 4

2 BS5588 *Fire precautions in the design and construction of buildings.* Part 8: Code of practice for means of escape for people with disabilities 1988

3 Loss Prevention Standard, Issue 1: *Code of practice - occupational fire brigades* Third draft (rev) 1991

4 *Storage of packaged dangerous substances* HSE Books 1992 ISBN 0 11 885989 7

5 *The assessment of fire hazards from solid materials and the precautions required for their safe storage and use. A guide for manufacturers, suppliers, storekeepers and users* HSE Books 1992 ISBN 0 11 885654 5

6 *Standard for the storage of roll paper* USA NFPA 231F National Fire Protection Association

7 Loss Prevention Council *Automatic sprinklers: design and installation* (Fire safety data PE11) 1985 National Fire Protection Association

8 *Keeping of LPG in cylinders and similar containers* HSE Books 1986 ISBN 0 7176 0631 7

9 *The safe use of acetylene in the pressure range 0-1.5 Bar* British Compressed Gas Association 1986

10 *The safe storage of gaseous hydrogen in seamless cylinders and other containers* Code of practice CP8 British Compressed Gas Association 1986

11 *Storage of LPG at fixed installations* HSE Books 1987 ISBN 0 11 883908 X

12 *Guide to dust explosion, prevention and protection* Parts 1-3 Institute of Chemical Engineers

13 BS 7430: 1991 *Code of practice for earthing*

14 BS EN 60529: 1992 *Specification for degrees of protection provided by enclosures* 1992

15 *Entry into confined spaces* HSE Books 1994 ISBN 0 7176 0787 9

16 BS 6133: 1985 *Code of practice for safe operation of lead-acid stationary cells and batteries*

17 *The storage of flammable liquids in fixed tanks (up to 10 000 m³ total capacity)* HSE Books 1990 ISBN 0 11 885532 8

18 *The storage of flammable liquids in containers* HSE Books 1990 ISBN 0 7176 0481 0

19 *The storage of flammable liquids in fixed tanks (exceeding 10 000 m³ capacity)* HSE Books 1991 ISBN 0 11 885538 7

20 *The safe use and handling of flammable liquids* HSE Books ISBN 0 7176 0967 7 (due for publication 1995)

21 BS 5345 *Code of practice for selection, installation and maintenance of electrical apparatus for use in potentially explosive atmospheres (other than mining applications of explosives processing and manufacture).* Part 1: *General recommendations* 1989; Part 2: *Classification of hazardous areas* 1983

22 *Diesel-engined lift trucks in hazardous areas* HSE Books 1986 ISBN 0 11 883535 1

23 *Memorandum of guidance on the Electricity at Work Regulations* 1989 HSE Books 1989 ISBN 0 11 883963 2

24 BS 5422: 1990 *Method for specifying thermal insulating materials on pipes, duct work and equipment (in the temperature range - 40°C to +700°C)*

25 BS 5970: 1992 *Code of practice for thermal insulation of pipework and equipment (in the temperature range - 100°C to +870°C)*

26 BS 5499 *Fire safety signs, notices and graphic symbols*, Part 1: *Specification for safety signs* 1990; Part 3: *Internally illustrated fire safety signs* 1991

27 *Hot work: welding and cutting on plant containing flammable materials* HSE Books 1979 ISBN 0 11 883229 8

28 BS 5588:1991 *Fire precautions in the design and construction of buildings* Part 10: *Code of practice for shopping complexes*

29 *Fire safety at work* Home Office and Scottish Office Home and Health Department HMSO 1989 ISBN 0 11 340905 2

30 BS5839: *Fire detection and alarm systems in buildings* Part 1: *Code of practice for system design, installation and servicing* 1988

31 *Gaseous fire extinguishing systems: precautions for toxic and asphyxiating hazards* HSE Books 1984 ISBN 0 11 883574 2

32 BS EN 2: 1992 *Classification of fires*

33 Building Regulations 1991: *Fire Safety approved document B5: Access and facilities for the Fire Service* Dept of the Environment 1991
ISBN 0 11 752313 5

34 Fire Precautions Act 1971, Ch 40, HMSO ISBN 0 10 544071 X

35 Health and Safety at Work etc Act 1974, Ch 37, HMSO ISBN 0 10 543774 3

36 *Code of practice for fire precautions in factories, offices, shops and railway premises not required to have a fire certificate* Home Office and Scottish Office Home and Health Department HMSO ISBN 0 11 340904 4

37 *Guide to the Health and Safety at Work etc Act 1974* HSE Books 1990
ISBN 0 7176 0441 1

38 *Reporting under RIDDOR* (HSE 24) HSE Books 1992 (free leaflet)

39 *Guide to the Dangerous Substances (Notification and Marking of Sites) Regulations 1990* HSE Books 1990 ISBN 0 11 885435 6

40 *CHIP 2 for everyone* - Chemicals (Hazard Information and Packaging for Supply) Regulations 1994 HSE Books 1995 ISBN 0 7176 0857 3

41 BS 5306: Part 3: *Fire extinguishing installations and equipment on premises*

42 BS 5274: 1985 *Specification for fire hose reels (water) for fixed installations*

43 BS 5423: 1987 *Specification for portable fire extinguishers*

44 BS 6575: 1985 *Specification for fire blankets*

45 BS 476 *Fire tests on building materials and structures*

46 BS5958 *Code of practice for control of undesirable static electricity.* Part 2: 1983 *Recommendations for particular industrial situations* ISBN 0 58 020018 3

47 *Electrostatic ignition - hazards of insulating materials* HSE Books 1982
ISBN 0 11 883629 3

48 *Fire safety in the printing industry* HSE Books 1992 ISBN 0 11 886375 4

Printed in the UK for the Health and Safety Executive   C20   7/95